*To*

_____

*From*

_____

*Date*

_____

*Message*

_____

_____

*A Little Book of Friendship*

Compiled from *The Glory of God's Grace, Fountains of Blessing, New Beginnings* and *A Voice Behind You* by Solly Ozrovech © by Christian Art Publishers.

© 2003 Christian Art Gifts, RSA
        Christian Art Gifts Inc., IL, USA

Compiled by Mairi-Ann Bonnet
Designed by Christian Art Gifts

Scripture taken from the *Holy Bible*, New International Version®. NIV®. Copyright © 1973, 1978, 1984 by International Bible Society. Used by permission of Zondervan Publishing House. All rights reserved.

Printed in Hong Kong

ISBN 1-86920-190-6

05  06  07  08  09  10  11  12  –  10  9  8  7  6  5  4  3

# A little book of

# *Friendship*

christian
art gifts

# Contents

# The

## friendship of Jesus

"You are my
friends if you do
what I command."
~ John 15:14

Christian disciples highly value the gift of friendship that Jesus offers to those who acknowledge His sovereignty. It is a gift of grace, something that you can never earn, but only accept. Christ very simply says, "I am your Friend. Will you accept this and treat Me as a friend that you love?"

If you accept this invitation, you submit to His loving discipline, because it is only in doing so that you can grow in the generous friendship that He offers you. True friendship with Jesus can be strengthened only by being in communion with Him and developing purer understanding of His love. Such communion and understanding is the result of a meaningful prayer life that is developed through complete obedience to your Lord.

The friendship that Jesus offers you can only become a reality if you submit yourself to His will. He knows what is best for you, and by obeying Him, you will realize that your Friend is your Guide through life.

# Making
## new friends

"Lord, you have
been our dwelling
place throughout all
generations ... from
everlasting to everlasting
you are God."

~ Psalm 90:1-2

You may have enjoyed the companionship of loved-ones and true friends for many years but gradually you realize that your circle of friends has begun to shrink. This world can suddenly and unexpectedly become a very lonely place as you grow older.

When you lose loved ones you must guard against becoming depressed. You might find yourself crying out in desperation, like Elijah, *"I am the only one left ... "* (1 Kgs. 19:10).

You must be willing to initiate new friendships without feeling that you are being disloyal to old ones.

Reconcile yourself to the fact that things have changed. Rejoice in sweet memories, but don't get caught up in them. Appreciate the knowledge that you gained from previous friendships and apply that knowledge to enrich new ones. Consciously search for opportunities to enrich the present, especially through friendships and relationships that God brings across your path.

# Thank God
## for friendship

"Jonathan, my brother,
you were very dear to
me. Your love for me
was wonderful,
more wonderful than
that of a woman."
~ 2 Samuel 1:26

A friend is someone whose company you enjoy and with whom you would like to spend eternity. You can depend on your friend when you go through hard times and he will rejoice with you when things go well.

You seek your friend's advice when you are worried, and welcome his congratulations when the problem is solved. You lean on him when your heart wants to break, but he never exploits your weakness.

You can cry on his shoulder when you are sad and laugh freely with him when you are happy. He admires your good qualities and loves you in spite of your weaknesses.

He is proud when you achieve your goals, but is not ashamed of you when you fail. He will speak the truth, even though it might hurt you; and you can be honest with him.

He will not hesitate to prove his friendship, even at the risk of being abused. He offers help without expecting anything in return. He will talk about the best in you when others talk about the worst.

# *Friendship*

## *under strain*

For Demas, because
he loved this world,
has deserted me
and has gone to
Thessalonica. Crescens
has gone to Galatia
and Titus to Dalmatia.
~ 2 Timothy 4:10

Nobody knows why Demas, Crescens and Titus left Paul. Neither do we know whether the separation was temporary or permanent. It is even possible for Christian friendships to be severely tested.

In the most intimate of human relations it is essential to respect personal privacy. Friends should not encroach upon the time you spend alone with God. Friendship can only thrive and grow in strength and beauty when we respect each other's individuality.

Prayer, love and openness are positive ways to relieve the tension in a relationship that experiences strain. Pray for God's blessing in the life of the person from whom you have become estranged. While praying you may discover something in your own life that has led to the tension. With His help you can possibly correct the misunderstanding. Prayer can rekindle the flame of friendship and love.

# " *I am*
## *sorry!* "

I confess my
iniquity; I am
troubled by my sin.
~ Psalm 38:18

"I am sorry!" are probably the hardest three words to say. Yet these three simple words can build bridges between estranged friends.

You might want to apologize to your friend, but find many reasons not to: you did nothing wrong; others will see you as weak; you will be humiliated; your friend will mock you when you offer your apology. So you avoid apologizing, yet deep inside you long to be able to say these healing words.

It is possible to pretend that your

broken friendship does not affect you, but you simply hide your hurt feelings. Where love and friendship once flourished, there is now much misunderstanding and recrimination. This might be because of your thoughtless words or ill-considered actions. Or you might not know why your friendship has cooled off.

If you apologize for the tension that has developed, you will enjoy the delight of a restored friendship. This is worth the effort of saying those three little words.

*"Tell me who your friends are ... "*

And David became more
and more powerful,
because the LORD
Almighty was with him.
~ 1 Chronicles 11:9

The old saying is clearly true, "Tell me who your friends are and I will tell you who you are." Some people still associate with their worldly friends after they have given their lives to Christ. They labor under the delusion that since their lives have changed, their friends will too. This very seldom occurs.

More often a new Christian will gradually revert to his old friends and their standards and eventually to his old way of life.

Once you have accepted Christ as

the Lord and King of your life, you should do everything in your power to strengthen your relationship with Him.

As you develop a meaningful relationship with Him you will have a greater understanding of other people. Your life will be filled with joy and you will attract new friends who also have a living relationship with Jesus Christ. As you seek Him in your fellowship with other believers, He will enrich your life with His glorious presence.

# *Give your friends space*

Seldom set foot in
your neighbor's house —
    too much of you,
and he will hate you.
    ~ Proverbs 25:17

One of God's most precious gifts to us is neighborliness and it should be nurtured and developed; it should not be taken for granted nor be placed under unnecessary strain.

Do not make the mistake of thinking that because you know people well you can allow yourself liberties that will restrict their freedom. They are entitled to times of privacy when they can be alone to lead their own lives.

People find joy in the company of others. However, they are also spiritual beings and need space to develop spiritually. Wise friends respect the privacy of their friends. However welcome you may be, never overstay your welcome.

Even within the intimacy of the family and marriage, respect for individual needs is of the utmost importance.

If someone wishes to be alone, do not think he is anti-social. He may be seriously coming to terms with God or himself.

# Convictions

## determine

## relationships

If it is possible, as
far as it depends on
you, live at peace
with everyone.
~ Romans 12:18

It is hard to respect someone who always agrees with everyone. But it is also extremely hard to live in peace with a person who is aggressive and always disagrees with anything that others say.

The ability to maintain strong convictions and yet keep the friendship and respect of those who differ from you becomes possible when you apply the basic principles of Christian love.

It is wise and admirable to have strong Christian convictions, but it is unwise to elevate those convictions to a form of pettiness and narrow-mindedness. You must be willing to listen to the viewpoint of others. If your convictions are true and stable, you have nothing to fear from the opinions of others. The key to edifying relationships is not to be found in uniformity of thought.

To have strong and reasonable convictions and yet not be narrow-minded, and to reveal love in your interpersonal relationships, shows that you are a disciple of the Master.

*Do you*

*have a human*

*relations program?*

How good and pleasant
it is when brothers
live together in unity!
~ Psalm 133:1

It is rewarding to understand people and to maintain healthy relationships with others. Sometimes this is relatively easy, but with some people it can be exceptionally difficult. So much depends on the disposition of other people: with some it is easy to start a conversation and their pleasant personalities make them a pleasure to be with. But not all people are like that.

There are many people who are abrupt and difficult and who seem to derive pleasure from making things unpleasant for those around them. If you ignore these people, you avoid the problem, but you do not solve it.

Handling the problem of human relations constructively requires patience and sympathetic understanding on your part. You need to give others the opportunity to talk even if what they say hurts. You need to remain calm. Then you will often discover that behind the rough exterior and apparent rudeness, there is a person who yearns for love and friendship.

*Let your*

*love be practical*

Dear children, let us
not love with words
or tongue but with
actions and in truth.
~ 1 John 3:18

True love is not something that can be fathomed by the human mind. It cannot be sufficiently explained, and yet it is the most important and vital human emotion.

Compassion, goodness, tenderness and many other beautiful and highly emotive words cannot succeed in describing the strength and power of love.

The foundation of true love is complete identification with the one who is loved. The same joys, sorrows, temptations and failures are experienced. True love entails sacrifice and often includes sadness. The quality of love transcends sympathy and comes to expression in loyalty and faithfulness, even if the whole world should turn against the be-loved.

Love in action is more than just the performance of good deeds. True love is unselfish and encompasses qualities such as faithfulness, trust and noble principles that enrich the mind and spirit. It cannot be bought, which is why love is so precious.

*Other books*

*in this range*

A little book of

*Hope*

ISBN: 1-86920-188-4

A little book of
*Joy*

ISBN: 1-86920-189-2

A little book of
*Promises*

ISBN: 1-86920-186-8

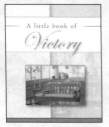

A little book of
*Victory*

ISBN: 1-86920-191-4

A little book of
*Wisdom*

ISBN: 1-86920-187-6